Courageous JOY

BOLDLY

STEP IN

STEP UP

& STEP OUT

IN YOUR FAITH

Julie McCarthy

Thank you for buying an authorized edition of this book.

Front Cover Photo Credit: Tatyana Consaul, Canva Pro
Editing: Susan C Young
Cover & Interior Design: Susan C Young

To invite Julie to speak at your next event,
Please email her at:
Julie.CourageousJoy@gmail.com

"I have known and lived life with Julie McCarthy for the past 25 years, and her heart for discipleship and seeing people walk in confident, joyful faith has never wavered. She has a way of communicating that inspires and brings insight into the truths of God's word. Her writing of Courageous Joy exemplifies her ability to share where true joy is found clearly and a roadmap to living in that joy as we courageously share with others. This book is a precious gift you will want to share with everyone you encounter."

—Mary Green
Worship/Communications Director, Hope Community Church

"Julie has lived a truly inspirational life. Her advice and counsel have always been most valuable. I'm confident the reader will find this book to be instructional and uplifting."

— June Streveler, Entrepreneur

*"I've known Julie for years, and she has always been such an inspiration to me. I love her outlook on life, devotion to her family, and strong faith in God. I was honored when Julie allowed me to help in a small way with this book, **Courageous Joy**! While reading it, I saw so much of her devotion and faith in her words. I was especially moved when reading about the "Meaning of Grace." The biblical meaning of grace reminds me that our God is truly wonderful! After reading Courageous Joy, I have decided to follow Julie's belief that it is important to make time for God every day first. It is too easy to say, "I don't have time" for Bible study or prayer. I was really touched by her heartfelt prayers, my favorite part being, "Help me spend my time with you first, to abide in you, so you can abide in me. Remind me that my time with you is a privilege!"*

—Chris Wetzel
Retired, Horse Enthusiast, Loving Friend

*"Julie McCarthy's book, **Courageous Joy**, is a delightful read and a powerful reminder that our walk with God can bring unlimited joy and possibility. When we have the courage to trust in the Lord and walk in faith, it can inspire us to transcend the troubles of this world and live a life of grace. Not only does Julie provide easy steps to follow, but she engages the reader by asking valuable questions to enrich our connection with the Holy Spirit."*

—Susan C Young
Keynote Speaker and Author of
'Release the Power of Re³: Building Resilience Through Challenge & Change and *'The Art of First Impressions for Positive Impact'*

"I cannot recommend this book more if you want to get real and raw with your faith. Julie will pull you in and give you incredible perspective. It will cause you to reflect and dive deeper into your faith. Knowing the peace God gives will strengthen your spiritual walk and bring joy to every day!"

—Leah McCarthy, Daughter-in-law

"In my work with hurting families, fear and hopelessness are recurring themes. The challenges of life have squeezed the joy from their lives. So many in our fast-paced world feel this way. I wish each one could sit down with my friend, Julie, and be encouraged by her joyous spirit and faith-filled words. Since this would be very difficult to do, her book, Courageous Joy, is the next best thing. Julie's love for the Lord and for you, dear reader, are bound within each page. Her message of hope is for you. Julie's story will turn your heart to the One who brings satisfying and eternal joy to the challenges of daily living."

—Tara Clark
Family Recovery Peer Specialist

Dedication

To my husband, Guy,
who has walked every step of this journey with me.
And to our children Thomas, Alyssa, Theresa, and Trevor
who continue to fill our hearts with joy every day.

A very special thank you to these faithful women
I'm blessed to call friends. Each has contributed
in a unique way, for which I am so grateful!

Angela Ackley
Tara Clark
Mary Green
Karen Screnock
June Streveler
Chris Wetzel
Susan C Young

Contents

Courageous JOY

BOLDLY

STEP IN

STEP UP

& STEP OUT

IN YOUR FAITH

Amy - you are a beautiful
woman of God.
So grateful for
you!

11

Welcome to Courageous Joy!

Introduction

A t the age of nineteen, on an unusually warm January day, I ventured out on my own horseback riding. I was cherishing the warmth of the sun on my face, the cool air, and the gentle sound of the leather saddle as it squeaked with every step. I was filled with gratitude for what seemed like a suspended moment in time, just for me. There's something so soothing and yet thrilling while riding horseback. The day seems to linger, take on a presence all its own. It allowed me to pause and take in all the beauty around me, so much so that I thought this was perhaps the best day ever! And then, I wondered, is this the fullness of life, moments like these?

As I pondered that thought, I prayerfully asked, "Lord, is this everything there is to life, or is there more? Am I missing something? Please show me." Discovering the answers to those questions transformed my life — forever! Now, decades later, I can honestly say that that was a pivotal moment in my life. I have discovered an abundant joy — beyond this world's delightful pleasures—surpassing all understanding. A joy all-encompassing, aside from circumstances, that I want to share with you. A joy that is life-changing!

The Merriam-Webster Dictionary defines joy as "the emotion evoked by well-being, success, good fortune or the prospect of possessing what one desires; the expression or exhibition of such emotion; a state of happiness or felicity; a source or cause of delight." On the surface, this is how the world perceives joy:

happiness achieved as a result of possessions, relationships, achievements, or financial success. However, there is a much more profound joy beyond all understanding that, yes, even defies circumstances. It is a joy that lies beneath the surface of our everyday lives — a joy that is longing to seep into our hearts, minds, and souls, a wellspring in our daily lives.

Joy is not just a feeling for a privileged or chosen few; it is available to all of us. In this book, I want to take you on a journey to gain insights, wisdom, clarity, and understanding, enabling you to embrace the wonder of a joy story yet to be told — yours! It doesn't matter what you've done or what you haven't done, who your family is or who your family isn't, where you come from, where you've gone, what you've said or what you haven't said. You are loved and not alone! Come along and discover for yourself the hidden treasure waiting for you to grasp, a treasure that no one can take away from you, no matter what is going on in your life today.

Now, all this may sound strange or even unattainable to you. But stay with me. I promise you will be glad you did! It is by design that we live in hope and joy!

Did you know that *joy* is addressed over 100 times in the Bible? Surprising, isn't it? I used to think the Bible was just a book of rules, of 'do this and don't do that.' So where, then, does joy fit in all that? I am so excited to show you!

It is possible to live in joy despite what the news tells us or whatever situation we find ourselves in today. How do we attain this joy, and why does it take courage? From where does courage come from?

Join me as we step into the truth, step up in our faith journey, and learn how to apply God's Word to our everyday lives so we can boldly step out into the world with courageous joy!

Let the journey begin . . .

Courageously
Step In

Courageous Joy

Step In

The Search for Joy

"You make known to me the path of life;
in your presence, there is fullness of joy;
to your right hand are pleasures forevermore."
Psalms 16:11

In the months following that memorable day of horseback riding, I went to a few Bible studies with a friend. One night, after attending my very first Bible study, I was driving home and singing out loud, freely enjoying the ability to belt out in song and not fear someone would judge my voice. As I sang one of the songs from that evening, Amazing Grace, I couldn't remember all the words. I innocently asked God aloud, "What are the rest of the words, Lord?" I paused, then reasoned again out loud, "Oh, well, you've probably heard enough of me, right, God?" So, I turned on the radio only to hear static. We lived out in the country, so that wasn't unusual. As I turned the dial to find a station, I heard a man's voice singing. The melody was familiar.

I held my breath in unbelief. Tears streamed warmly down my cheeks as the words became clear—it was a man singing Amazing Grace! And there it was, the very first time I ever encountered God's presence so powerfully. As I sat in unbelief and bewilderment, I choked out, "Oh, God, you're really here!" More tears, sobbing at this point . . . How could it be? Did He REALLY hear me on this dark summer night while driving out in the country? God revealed Himself to me like never before. He IS real. He *more than* answered my innocent Prayer, asking for the words to that song. He HADN'T heard enough from me. He cared deeply about my simple request and wanted me to know beyond a shadow of a doubt that He was here. He cares. He listens. And yes, there is MUCH more to life than I ever knew!

God shows up in even the smallest details of life.

Every day, we see people who appear sad, discouraged, and hopeless. In fact, if we look around, we see a lot of them. It seems to be more common than not that people take for granted what appears to them like just another day in this life: the demands of the 9 to 5 grind, late-night worries, the tending to children with selfless surrendering to their every need, the spilled milk, relationship rifts. The list goes on. I remember going about my day, and someone asked me, "How are you doing today?" I responded, "Great, thanks!" And he retorted jokingly, "Well, tell your face!" Eek! That was a wake-up call! How did I get myself into such a dither of taking care of daily business that a passerby saw fatigue and joylessness on my face? Maybe that's where you find yourself now. Give yourself a break and know that it happens to all of us. But the good news is, we don't have to stay there!

Have you also noticed when we see someone whose heart and face are filled with joy, we stop and take notice, don't we? A smile is an international language where no interpreter is needed. It's contagious. In that brief moment in time, we sense a whisper of hope in the world that all will be okay.

When we have a daily appreciation for the bountiful blessings all around us, we are often smiling in such a way that it invites others to join us in the delight of the day. There is a magnetic effect that draws people near to us. There's a contagious transfer of joy.

We're naturally drawn to joyful people for their positivity, optimistic outlook, and simple pleasure in everyday life. Ah . . . to live with so much joy that it lifts our steps! But is it that easy? Not by a long shot!

What is the key to this joy? Why, in this day, when so many of our daily needs are met, do we find ourselves with a long face, downtrodden heart, entangled in the burdens of this life?

Interestingly, the Institute for Global Ethics conducted interviews with former heads of state, professors, activists, business executives, writers, and religious figures from many nations. Rushworth Kidder and his colleagues asked, "If you could help create a global code of ethics, what would be in it?" Their research revealed eight global values that transcend countries, cultures, and traditions. Here are their findings on these global values:

1. Love
2. Truthfulness
3. Fairness
4. Freedom
5. Unity
6. Tolerance
7. Responsibility
8. Respect for Life

It's reasonable to assume that if a person were to attain all these values at once, they would indeed lead a happy and fulfilled life. However, in today's challenging world, where these values are continuously tested, how can one live with joy despite their absence?

Take a moment to consider what brings you joy.

God created you in your mother's womb; unique, one of a kind, beautiful, and precious in His sight. What are the things He has placed in your heart and life that bring you joy? Write notes in the Reflection Questions in the back of each section or on a separate piece of paper. These are important! We will come back to this.

"Spiritual Bank Account"— What?

"For we are His workmanship, created in Christ Jesus for good works, which God prepared beforehand, that we should walk in them."
Ephesians 2:10

While growing up, I always felt a silent, hidden insecurity, wondering whether or not I could be "good enough" in this life. (News flash — I'm not!) I feared the heavy hand of God (as I perceived it to be) would come down and punish me if I didn't measure up. Yes, my fear was real! I'd heard varying schools of thought regarding this. A common assumption is that if you are a good person, you will automatically gain entry into Heaven—that good works and good deeds are enough to *earn* the ultimate reward of Heaven. Let me caution you here – that couldn't be further from the truth! However, if you, like me, were taught this growing up, I have great news for you!

I remember packing up our young family and driving down to Northern Illinois, where I grew up, as we often traveled for holidays to be with family and give our children time with their grandparents. But this time, it was for my grandmother's funeral.

At this point in my life, I had read much of the Bible for myself, worked through Bible studies, and had come to challenge the 'religion' of my upbringing. It was a bit surreal, sitting there at my grandmother's funeral, at the same altar where my husband and I were married years earlier and said our marriage vows.

Taking in the moment, I was caught off guard as the priest, while he gave my grandmother's eulogy, used a metaphor that I remember to this day — not because it was profound, but rather quite unsettling! He attempted to give an example of how we might earn our way to Heaven someday. He went on to say, "Life is like a bank account, made of deposits (good deeds) and withdrawals (sins) and at the end of it . . ." he went on and lifted his hands in the air at different heights and then alternated them up and down asking, "Where does your balance fall?" That, in his estimation, settled a person's eternal destiny, where they ended up on one side or the other as in a double pan scale. My heart sank. This did *not* represent God's truth. Stay with me here — there's good news just ahead! Unfortunately, there are some who will trouble us and distort the truth. But know this – there is no one who lives up to God's standard of perfection. NO ONE. We are in trouble. We need a Savior.

Finding Faith

"Now faith is the assurance of things hoped for,
the conviction of things not seen."
Hebrews 11:1

And that Savior is Jesus. Just Jesus. The one who was born of the Virgin Mary, lived among us for over 30 years and taught us patiently how God wants us to live, all while leading a sinless life himself. Those who were in power hated Jesus. They were jealous of his following and considered him a threat. He was condemned to death on a cross. There he died and three days later was raised up back to life, the resurrection that had been foretold centuries earlier. He was seen by over 500 of his followers in the days following, bearing the holes in his hands and feet and the gash in his side where he was speared.

And so it was established, from the beginning of time, when God ordered one final atonement for sin, that He would send his only Son to bear the cross, to die, once and for all, for ALL our sins. It is finished by placing your faith in Jesus. How? The simplest way to tell you is just as it is written in the book of Romans. "The word is near you; It is in your mouth and in your heart." That is, the Word of Faith we are proclaiming; profess "Jesus is Lord," and believe in your heart that God raised him from the dead, and you will be saved. For it is with your heart that you believe and are justified, and with your Prayer that you profess and are saved. As the scripture says, "Anyone who trusts in him will never be put to shame." For there is no difference between Jew and Gentile – the same Lord is Lord of all and richly blesses all who call on him, for "Everyone who calls on the name of the Lord will be saved."

Hold everything! For real? Yes! When I first came to this realization, I was beside myself! I had held myself captive by my fears and misbelief throughout my childhood and teen years by thinking my salvation was in my own hands and doing! Given their actions, words, or misdeeds, I was convinced that not many had a chance to go to Heaven. I became judgmental, self-righteous, and even cynical. I think of the times when I judged, sneered, and even became shamefully proud of my actions and inactions. I cringe, looking back at the times when I spoke out, while I should have bitten my tongue and kept my mouth shut! (It still happens. I'm a work in progress— sigh) I thought I was SO right, so sure . . . but I wasn't.

And here's the most important part you need to hear. Notice we're told "**anyone**" who trusts in him and "**everyone**" who calls on the name of the Lord will be saved. Isn't this incredible? Comforting? Loving? Forgiving? Reassuring! I stand in awe when I think of the sacrifice Jesus made for me, for you, our sins, and our loved ones who have placed their trust in Him.

Honestly, what a relief! I know I could never do or say everything I should and avoid everything I shouldn't do. I am a work in progress, and I fall short every day of what my 'perfect' self would do or not do. We all work toward being a better self than we were the day before. But with God's grace (forgiveness) and His written Word, we have been provided wisdom, comfort, encouragement, and guidance — more than any earthly being could ever provide. Okay, so if Jesus was so great, why then did He have to die on the cross?

Now, that's one core detail to this familiar story of Jesus that most of you may already know. After all, the story started well over 2000 years ago, recorded in God's inspired Word in the Bible, and has passed through the ages. I'm not sure how I missed this integral piece of history leading up to our salvation, but I did! Have you ever gone along for a while, thinking you knew the whole story, the truth, and accepted it as truth; however, there was one more element to the story that you learned much further down the road where all the pieces came together like a puzzle that had been missing just a few — but very important — pieces? Let me share with you what I missed.

Despite all my Sundays in church growing up (which were actually a bit few and far between), I never quite understood why Jesus was referred to as the Lamb of God. Do you? Perhaps I accepted it without question because a lamb appears gentle, peaceful, and white. Sure, I guess a lamb was fitting.

You see, according to God's law, long before Jesus was born, in order for the Jews to be cleansed from their sins, they were to bring a goat or a lamb, one without blemish, to be sacrificed as a sin offering. The individual who committed a sin "must bring as his offering a male goat without defect. He is to lay his hand on the goat's head and slaughter it, which served as a sin offering. Sometimes, it was a female goat, bull, or lamb, but it was always to be one without defect. According to God's law, when sinners lay their hands on the head of the unblemished goat, their sins were transferred to the goat. Then, the priest would burn it on the altar. In this way, the priest made atonement (forgiveness of sins) for them, and they were forgiven. Gasp!

As you can imagine, this was a harrowing reality, but at that time, that is what God established in order to receive atonement for one's sins. I can hardly imagine the ceremonial undertaking this was. And then further, to even comprehend the anguish, "for God so loved the world that he gave his one and only Son, that whoever believes in him shall not perish but have eternal life." (John 3:16) Jesus became the one final sacrifice for all sins of those who placed their faith in Him. He was perfect, without defect or sin. He is the only person who has ever lived on this earth without sinning. Yes, He was the perfect, unblemished

26

Lamb of God. Jesus chose to die for us rather than give up on us! He died in our place so we wouldn't receive the fate we deserve as sinners.

Surely, if someone could be a good enough person to go to Heaven as a result of one's own efforts and good deeds, then Jesus wouldn't have had to die on the cross! Trust me when I say this was a hard thing for me to wrap my head around, but it is in this message that the truth resides. Oh, please hear me when I tell you, dear ones, no one — I mean, no one — can be good enough, do enough good works, say the right things, or give enough money to go to Heaven on their own accord. Rather, it is by God's grace — unearned and undeserved favor — through our faith in Jesus that our sins are forgiven.

Meaning of Grace

"For by grace you have been saved through faith. And this is not of your own doing; it is the gift of God, not a result of works, so that no one may boast."
Ephesians 2:8

Let's talk about grace. Its meaning deserves clarity, especially since this Word has two meanings. One is the familiar meaning associated with simple elegance or movement, as how we would expect to see a ballerina be graceful. But the more significant meaning of the Word grace is biblical. In the Bible, grace refers to God's forgiveness of our sins, undeserved and unearned, freely given by God to those who place their faith in Jesus. By God's grace alone, we are forgiven.

What about all of our good works? After all, we're taught throughout God's Word to do good deeds, to love and serve others. In Ephesians, Paul explains, "For by grace you have been saved through faith. And this is *not your own doing*; it is the gift of God, *not a result of works*, so that no one may boast. For we are his workmanship, created in Christ Jesus for good works, which God prepared beforehand that we should walk in them" (Ephesians 2:8-10, italics added). Therefore, our good works, as God commands us to do, are out of gratitude for the grace we've been given out of the obedience we're called to.

But isn't that too easy? What about the Ten Commandments? And what about all the teachings from Jesus about how to live out our days on this earth? Are they not God's law anymore?

Just because we know we receive forgiveness for our sins doesn't mean that we can go on and continue to sin, knowing that we can be forgiven for them. No, as we turn our hearts toward Jesus, we learn about the way he wants us to choose to live out our lives here on earth. Through His Word, He guides us in the decisions that we make. He protects us. He counsels us and consoles us. Our hearts begin to change and become more like the heart of Jesus. We are forever changed when we invite Jesus into our hearts, and it is in knowing him that a wellspring of joy begins to spring forth from our being — both in our thoughts and words, in our actions and relationships.

I remember as a mom homeschooling my children for the first time, my mouth got the better of me. Boy, could I yell! That was *not* how I wanted our days to go! I remember when I found a verse that convicted me of my tone and yelling, so I wrote it out on an index card and taped it up on my bathroom mirror. I was reminded of it before I even left the room to greet my children in the morning. The verse read, "Do not let any unwholesome talk come out of your mouth, but only what is helpful for building others up according to their needs that it may benefit those who listen." Oh, boy. I know all my words were not beneficial, and they did not build them up! I wasn't a terrible mom; I was actually, I think, a pretty great mom! But I can tell you I had my moments! Even now, so many years later, I can almost recite that verse from memory. It took me a while, but I learned to heed God's Word, and did it ever make a difference in our days!

Moments like these exhibit our need for grace. We are all born as sinners, and I'm certainly no exception! As I drew nearer to God and read more of His words to us in the Bible, I became more aware of my own sinful nature. But I was also humbly reminded how we are forgiven and — just as importantly — how we are called to extend forgiveness to others in our daily lives.

The Truth Foretold

"Therefore the Lord himself will give you a sign. Behold, the virgin shall conceive and bear a Son and shall call his name Immanuel."
Isaiah 7:14

The coming of a Savior was foretold hundreds of times in the Old Testament. For those of you who are new to the Bible, it is in two parts: the Old Testament, which is from before Jesus was born, and the New Testament, which begins at Jesus' birth. Around 700 years before Jesus was born, Isaiah prophesied, "Therefore, the Lord himself will give you a sign. Behold, the virgin shall conceive and bear a Son and shall call his name Immanuel." (Isaiah 7:14) Details of Jesus' life and death are foretold beyond reproof throughout the Old Testament. Only through a powerful almighty God could there be such an accurate account and summation of what would lie *hundreds of years* ahead! We read in the Old Testament, in the book of Isaiah, chapter nine:

"For to us a child is born,
to us a son is given;
and the government shall be upon his shoulder,
and his name shall be called
Wonderful Counselor, Mighty God,
Everlasting Father, Prince of Peace.
Of the increase of his government and of peace
there will be no end,
on the throne of David and over his kingdom,
to establish it and to uphold it
with justice and with righteousness
from this time forth and forevermore.
The zeal of the Lord of hosts will do this." – Isaiah 9:6-7

And in the book of Zechariah 9:9:

"Rejoice greatly, O daughter of Zion!
Shout aloud, O daughter of Jerusalem!
Behold, your king is coming to you;
righteous and having salvation is he,
humble and mounted on a donkey,
on a colt, the foal of a donkey."

And revealingly, also foretold in Isaiah:

"He was despised and rejected by men,
a man of sorrows and acquainted with grief;
and as one from whom men hide their faces
he was despised, and we esteemed him not.

Surely, he has borne our griefs
and carried our sorrows;
yet we esteemed him stricken,
smitten by God, and afflicted.
But he was pierced for our transgressions;
he was crushed for our iniquities;
upon him was the chastisement that brought us peace,
and with his wounds we are healed." (Isaiah 53:3-5)

And then, over 700 years later, it came to be . . .

His mother, Mary, wept at the foot of her son's cross in despair and anguish, as only a mother could do. You see, the Jewish religious leaders didn't recognize Jesus as the one whom God promised was to come. Here he was in the flesh totally man as they were, yet totally God — just as the scriptures foretold. The one they were waiting for. The promised Savior! God's own son, Jesus of Nazareth. The one who performed mighty works and wonders and signs that God did through him, in their midst. Instead of recognizing him for who he was, the leaders became jealous of his following. He drew large crowds when he spoke. He ate with sinners and had compassion for them. He lived a blameless life of perfection, teaching only love and forgiveness. Yet here he was, beaten, stripped, spat on, insulted, and nailed to a cross like that of a criminal.

And then the final hour arrived; darkness came over the whole land, for the sun stopped shining for three hours. The earth shook, and rocks were split. And Jesus called out with a loud voice, "Father, into your hands I commit my spirit." When He said this, He had breathed his last. When many who were there "saw the earthquake and what took place, they were filled with awe and said, "Truly this was the Son of God!'" (Matthew 27:54 ESV). It was finished — the ultimate sacrifice for our sins. Then, just as the prophets foretold centuries earlier, He rose after three days! And yes, he walked and talked with many in the days following!

A few years ago, I was busy preparing for Easter weekend with my family due to arrive in a few hours. My oldest son is quite crafty when it comes to creating things out of wood, so I had asked him to make me a cross. I then found a decorative scrolled metal cross to overlay it. My daughter helped me as we took some nails and attached them to both sides of the cross and the bottom. We each drew a long breath and looked at each other as we were overcome with compassion and solemn hearts, for it was Good Friday. The nails we hammered were where Jesus' hands and feet were nailed to the cross . . . physically, a gut-wrenching response, fully taking in the weight of my sin, and why Jesus died on the cross — to be the ONE, the final sacrifice for ALL of our sins, for those who accept this salvation through faith in Him.

If you have not placed your faith in Christ, commence your journey to the path of everlasting joy. Submit your life to Christ. I encourage you to step in with faith, laying the foundation for the joy no person or circumstance can ever rob you of! We're told in Luke 15:7, "I tell you that in the same way there will be more rejoicing in heaven over one sinner who repents than over ninety-nine righteous persons who do not need to repent."

Let eternal love come into your life. Profess your faith in Jesus, God's only Son who died on the cross for you! Accept Him into your heart. Many who walked with Jesus on this earth witnessed His death on the cross. Following His resurrection, hundreds of people saw Him, and all profess — He IS the Son of God, who was raised up on the third day and lives today in Heaven. And even though you and I cannot see Him, He is as alive today as he was then and cares deeply about you.

"For God so loved the world that he gave his one and only Son, that whoever believes in him shall not perish but have eternal life." (John 3:16) God's love and grace through Jesus is the source of our hope; and from hope, comes peace; and from peace, comes joy. Whatever your past may hold, no matter how broken you may feel today, God is waiting with open arms for you to go to Him. Surrender, and ask Him to be the Lord of your life.

My heart aches solemnly for what Jesus had to endure for our sins, for the sins of this world, including mine and yours, to serve as the sacrificial lamb without blemish for our sins! Pause here and reflect on how Jesus died for you. He put himself in our place and endured the punishment and shame for *our* sins! If you have not prayed for Jesus to enter your heart and place your faith in him, you can do so now. He is waiting with open arms for you, His child, whom he knit together in your mother's womb. He loves you dearly and is aching for you to place your faith in Him!

Pruyer

Prayer

Suggested Prayer to invite Jesus into your heart:

All praise and honor and glory to you, Lord! You are the one true God who sent your Son to die for my sins so that I may have eternal life with you. I submit to you, Lord, and place my faith in Jesus. Please forgive me for my sins.

Thank you, Lord, for your promise. Lord, help me daily to remember your sacrifice and the depth of your love for me. "I pray that out of your glorious riches may you strengthen me with power through your Spirit in my inner being so that Christ may dwell in my heart through faith.

Being rooted and established in love, may I have power, together with all the Lord's holy people, to grasp how wide and long and high and deep is the love of Christ and to know this love that surpasses knowledge—that I may be filled to the measure of all the fullness of God." (Ephesians 3:16-19)

Oh, Heavenly Father, have mercy on me. Thank you for the sacrifice you made through Jesus' death on the cross for me! Please come into my heart as I place my faith in you. Please show me your will and teach me your ways. Open my eyes and let me see the glorious joy you have in store for me.

Amen.

Reflection Questions

What has God placed in your heart and life that brings you joy?

_____

_____

_____

_____

What myths or beliefs have been clarified or shed light on that may have been stealing your joy?

_____

_____

_____

_____

What promises from God's Word are speaking to your heart?

_____

_____

_____

_____

Courageously
Step Up

Step Up

By Faith, Not by Sight

". . . for we walk by faith, not by sight."
2 Corinthians 5:7

One day, when my Dad was telling one of his usual entertaining stretches of truth, he jokingly asked me, "What are you, a doubting Thomas?" He was often hilarious with what he could come up with! But then I asked him, "Do you even know where that phrase came from?" He's like, "Yeah, you know when someone doesn't believe you, they're a 'doubting Thomas'!" It was fun to share with him.

On the evening of the first day of the week after Jesus' death and resurrection, the disciples were meeting with the doors locked for fear of the Jewish leaders. But even though the doors were locked, "Jesus came and stood among them and said to them, 'Peace be with you!' When He said this, He showed them his hands and his side." They were overjoyed to see Him! However, the disciple Thomas, one of the twelve, was not present that evening. He did not believe the others when they told him they had seen the Lord.

"Eight days later, his disciples were inside again, and Thomas was with them. Although the doors were locked, Jesus came and stood among them and said, 'Peace be with you.' Then He said to Thomas, "Put your finger here and see my hands; and put out your hand, and place it in my side. Do not disbelieve, but believe." Thomas answered Him, "My Lord and my God!" Jesus said to him, "Have you believed because you have seen me? Blessed are those who have not seen and yet have believed." (John 20:26-29)

There were times when I felt just like Thomas did. "Yeah, right. That wasn't Jesus. It was just a coincidence," I would tell myself. Well, I've learned to eat my words! He is here, and He is real! Let me share a life-changing moment when the Lord stepped into our lives, and we boldly proceeded in faith alone to follow His lead!

When God Shows Up in Unexpected Places

". . . fear not, for I am with you; be not dismayed, for I am your God; I will strengthen you, I will help you, I will uphold you with my righteous right hand."
Isiah 41:10

Many years ago, February of 1998 to be exact, while we were living in La Crosse, Wisconsin, we took what one would call a leap of faith. My husband and I had often talked about the possibility of someday moving up north to enjoy a simpler daily life without all the hustle and bustle. We longed for simpler days with more opportunities to enjoy the lakes, as we had previous summers while on short vacations in Northern Wisconsin. Life was certainly hectic with our four small children — three in elementary school and a toddler. I had started my own custom embroidery business and had a few employees. When my husband, Guy, often came home from work, I would 'pass the baton' to him to take care of the kids while I returned to work.

One day, my four-year-old gave me a wake-up call after I had *finally* decided to clear off the mound of paperwork on the dining room table, polish it, and put a vase of flowers in the middle. She turned to me and innocently asked, "Mommy, who wrecked your *message table*?" What? Really? It was then that my husband and I started to share our prayers of finding a more family-friendly way of life with each other. Our neighbor, who had been homeschooling her children, was an inspiration to me. Was this perhaps something we could do? What was God's will for us? Surely, it wasn't the hectic lifestyle that we'd fallen into.

I remember one morning while in the bathroom brushing my hair, ready to rush out the door, when my husband spoke up from the shower. "There's a job opening up north . . . should I ask about it?" Hardly believing my ears, I asked him if he was serious, and he assured me he was. I said, "Sure!" and rushed on my way. When he arrived at work, his boss stopped in and told him he could have that job, but they'd have to know his decision by the end of the following week because they needed to fill that position. Then began two weeks of fervent prayer asking for God's wisdom and guidance, for we had not only our house to sell (which we already had for sale for a year), but also my embroidery business to sell! "Please, God, give us a VERY clear answer – and please, God, in black and white so I don't miss it!"

The following Thursday evening was not just another busy week coming to a close but rather a very important night for us to discuss and make a final decision as to whether he should accept this new position. We were rushing to get the kids settled for the night, telling them, "Mommy and Daddy have important talking to do tonight!" What happened next is, to this day, the most memorable faith moment for us! Guy was helping our oldest with his math at the kitchen table. When I opened my daughter's backpack and pulled out her second-grade spelling list, I gasped as we hadn't practiced her words all week, and tomorrow would be her test. As I glanced at the list of words, it struck me oddly that they were handwritten and not typed out as they had been all school year. I began to read the list of words: turn, here, why, ask, read, need, land, different, home, us, move, try. I couldn't believe my eyes!

"Guy, look at this!" I exclaimed. "Wait, let me finish this." "No!" I interrupted, "You NEED to see this. You're not going to believe it!" He got up from the table, looked at the list, and I still remember him thrusting his hand to his head in disbelief, "This is it! This is the answer we've been praying for!" We knew immediately what the Lord wanted us to do. Decision made! How mighty is our God, who shows up in the simplest of forms, even through a spelling list!

The following five months were a bit stressful: trying to sell our house, finding a buyer for my business, and, of course, taking care of our four children amidst all of this while Guy was gone all week, back home only on the weekends due to the distance. We knew the Lord would help us take care of the details, and He did! We sold both our house and my business, and we moved to northern Wisconsin to a house across the street from a beautiful lake. We found a church that brought God's truth to light, and we grew ever so close as a family. As surely as you are reading this today, God is waiting for you to turn to Him, ask Him for guidance, and trust Him. "And I tell you, ask and it will be given to you; seek, and you will find; knock, and it will be opened to you. For everyone who asks, receives; and the one who seeks, finds; and to the one who knocks, it will be opened." (Luke 11:9)

Prayer

Praise to you, Lord. You are all-knowing. Thank you for your steadfast love and for the promptings you put in my heart.

Forgive me, Lord, for times when I turned away from you, have gone my own way filled with pride or self-sufficiency, doubt, and fear when all along it is only through you that I may be holy and righteous in your sight. Give me strength, wisdom, and discernment, Lord, as I walk in these troubled days with mixed messages all around me. Guide me in the way of obedience. May your Holy Spirit nudge me in the direction I should go. Help me to seek your will first for me. Cast light on each new step I should take.

Help me to boldly step up in my faith and follow your leadership. All strength, honor, and glory are yours alone, Lord. I pray in your precious Son's name, Jesus.

Amen.

Imperishable Seeds

"Light is sown for the righteous, and joy for the upright in heart."

Psalm 97:11

Pausing to look out our window on an early cool spring morning, my husband was already outside preparing to plant our garden. Curious, though exciting, isn't it? We cheerfully put effort into something we're passionate about, all in anticipation of the promise of what is to come. One can only imagine our Lord's anticipation as he sowed His seeds in us through His inspired Word! Beginning in the Old Testament and continuing in the New Testament, God's Word, through the writings of the Disciples, recorded as they walked alongside Jesus over 2,000 years ago, is still alive and thriving today!

In a garden, seeds planted and left unnourished may wither and die over time as they are perishable when left untended. However, when seeds are cultivated through the rich soil, with rain from above and the nurturing care of the gardener, new life springs forth. Similarly, seeds of hope, planted in us at the dawn of our faith, are cultivated through God's inspired Word and His gift of the Holy Spirit who dwells within us. We are assured of this undying love as written in 1 Peter 1:23: "The seeds cultivated in us, however, will not wither and die over time, "since you have been born again, not of perishable seed but of imperishable, through the living and abiding word of God." (Hint: When reading the Bible, take special note when you see a word that ends in *'ing.'* It reveals an active, ongoing state, such as the "living and abiding word of God.")

44

I remember when I was in a Bible study with other moms. While the kids were back in school, we were studying 'The Hall of Faith,' as it's called. It's about all the actions of heroes of the Bible – fueled by faith – in Hebrews Chapter 10. I came across a verse that jumped off the page, Hebrews 10:14: "For by one sacrifice he has made perfect forever those who are *being made* holy." (Italics mine). Ah, it is a process! It says those who are *BEING MADE* holy, not 'those who are already holy'! Thank goodness! I'm still a work in progress, and I appreciated knowing that I'm 'being' made holy – I'm not there yet. It's a process I'm still learning and will continue to. Be patient with yourself. See how the farmer waits for the land to yield its valuable crop and how patiently he waits for the autumn and spring rains. You, too, be patient. Draw near to the Lord, and He will draw near to you! We are not perfect, but He is perfect.

Fertile Hearts

"But the fruit of the spirit is love, joy, peace, patience, kindness, goodness, faithfulness, gentleness, self-control; against such things, there is no law."
Galatians 5:22-23

How, then, do we keep the soil of our hearts and our minds rich and fertile for the cultivating of God's Word and the working of the Holy Spirit active in our lives? One way is by regularly reading God's Word in the Bible, even if it's just a small passage a day. Scripture informs and cultivates our hearts in a way that no other writing has ever done or will do. It's the true essence of how He wants us to live our lives and experience the true joy that he has designed for us. It is also important to enter into fellowship (friendship with other Christians). We are called to continue to gather together. "As iron sharpens iron, so one person sharpens another." (Proverbs 27:17) I have been blessed by some incredible friendships over the years, but there are a small few who I can share and learn from, glean from their wisdom, pray with them, and support one another as we travel through life together.

We were made for fellowship with Christian friends to share in each others' burdens and joys. I pray you find a church with Bible-based teaching. Attend a Christian-based women's event in your area, or reach out and volunteer. Having fellow Christian friends is very important. Think of what Mary did after the angel appeared to her telling her she would conceive and bear a son, and he would be named Jesus — she "rose and went with haste to the hill country," where she ran to tell Elizabeth!

When we actively pursue learning and reading and sharing our faith with others, there is a natural joy and confidence that seeps into our everyday lives. There are so many golden nuggets of wisdom to be discovered. Lean in, read, ask, seek, and find the goodness of the Lord. When God opens our eyes, our faith turns to belief. Our belief turns to trust. Our trust ushers in peace. And peace brings joy.

One of my favorite verses in the Bible is referred to as 'The Fruit of the Spirit'—"But the fruit of the spirit is love, joy, peace, patience, kindness, goodness, faithfulness, gentleness, self-control; against such things, there is no law." (Galatians 5:22-23) Who doesn't want all of that? And how do we produce this fruit in our lives?

As we draw near to God, He draws near to us. The Holy Spirit grows this fruit in us as we abide in Christ Jesus. It is the work of God, as we grow in our relationship with him, that we begin to recognize the fruit of the Spirit in our lives. Jesus teaches us an invaluable lesson regarding our connection with Him, as remaining in the vine. "I am the true vine, and my Father is the vinedresser. Every branch in me that does not bear fruit he takes away, and every branch that does bear fruit he prunes, that it may bear more fruit." (John 15:1) Notice here Jesus refers to how a gardener prunes branches, to bear *more* fruit. An avid gardener will tell you that it is necessary to prune a tree to enable more air and sunlight to reach the full plant, reduce the chance for diseased branches, and help prevent insect and decay organisms from affecting the overall tree. Similarly, sometimes God prunes us! Have you ever experienced something that caused pain or a feeling of loss at the time, but then later on, it became a blessing in disguise?

Jesus continues. "Already you are clean because of the Word that I have spoken to you. Abide in me, and I in you. As the branch cannot bear fruit by itself unless it abides in the vine, neither can you unless you abide in me." I love to pull out my Bible and read with a highlighter and a pen. I will mark those verses that have come to me just at the time that I needed to hear them. It's funny how it works that way. I even find that when I listen to Christian radio. When I'm going through a trying time, sure enough, a song pops on the radio, and poof, there's the Word of encouragement and truth I needed to hear!

Abide

"I am the vine; you are the branches.
Whoever abides in me and I in him, he it is that bears much
fruit, for apart from me you can do nothing."
John 15:5

A bide. What does that really mean? The word 'abide' is a verb, meaning to accept or act in accordance with a rule, decision, or recommendation. Words such as dwell, remain, continue, and stay are used in defining abide. It's a complex yet simple concept. Abiding in Christ is not a feeling or a belief, but rather something we do, an action. Jesus appoints each of us to be His disciples and empowers and equips us to *abide* in Him so that He can *abide in us*! Incredible, isn't it?

How often do we cry out to the Lord, asking Him for guidance, comfort, understanding, peace, or even a miracle? He has made himself completely available to us through His Word 24/7! If to abide in Him is what He asks — *so that* He can abide in us — why would we neglect to turn to His inspired Word and simply abide? Especially as we read what's next. "As the Father has loved me, so have I loved you. Abide in my love. If you keep my commandments, you will abide in my love, just as I have kept my Father's commandments and abide in his love. These things I have spoken to you, that my **joy may be in you**, and that **your joy may be full**." (Bolded lettering mine) Read that again! We were created to be filled with JOY!

Recently, heavy storms came through. As I picked up all the broken sticks and fallen twigs, I was reminded of Jesus' Word — abide. I'll never forget the words from a dear friend who commented, "If I miss my morning time with the Lord, I feel like I've been deprived for the rest of the day!" Maybe you already know that feeling. I know I sure do when I don't carve out quiet time with God to read His Word and pray. The day tends to slip by with unfinished work and misspoken words, insecurity, and sapped of joy. You are God's dearly beloved. Let me encourage you, dear friends: I have seen God's work at hand – it's amazing! Step up in your faith journey by absorbing God's Word, letting his Words of love, encouragement, forgiveness, promise, hope, joy, and everlasting peace seep into your very being. The richness of your life will envelop you in a new hope with abundant joy. When it seems like I don't have enough time in the day, but still spend time to be with the Lord, it's like He pauses time for me! There is no rushing. It's almost as if time has multiplied!

Think for a moment of a child that is dear to you. If they were to crawl up on your lap and seek guidance and comfort from you, wouldn't you do whatever you could to be there for them? Of course you would! In the same way, our Heavenly Father is here waiting for you to turn to Him. Call out to Him. Jesus, oh, the precious name of Jesus! He is there and waiting for you. Read from the book He wrote to inspire and teach us how to live out these days. Abide in Him. Pour a cup of coffee, sit, and ponder his words. Kneel in Prayer. There's something deep that happens when we kneel and pray to our Heavenly Father. He listens. He cares. He moves. He loves. He forgives. He nurtures. He lights the next step. He counsels us, comforts us. He brings us peace. And all this brings a wellspring of joy to our days!

Prayer

Lord, help me to remember that the most important time of the day is the time I spend with you. In my crazy, busy days, I rush about doing all the things I have to do; meeting my daily expectations, working, caring for my family, loved ones and friends, keeping up my household, etc., and often neglecting the rest. It is so easy to resolve in thought "I don't have time." But I trust You, Lord. Help me spend my time with you first, to abide in you, so you can abide in me.

Remind me that my time with you is a privilege! We get to spend time alone with our creator, the One who placed the desires in my heart, the one who knows of my coming and going, even the number of hairs on my head. You know my every need even before I ask. You wait patiently for me to turn my eyes toward you.

Lord, bless the timing of my days. Help me to glorify you as you strengthen me through the power of your Holy Spirit in my inner being. Help me to tend to the soil of my heart, keeping it fertile and well-nourished with your Word, to abide in You so that you, Lord, can abide in me.

Amen

But Sometimes It's So Hard!

"For I am sure that neither death nor life, nor angels nor rulers, nor things present nor things to come, nor powers, nor height nor depth, nor anything else in all creation, will be able to separate us from the love of God in Christ Jesus our Lord."

Romans 8:38-39

You might be thinking, *"But you don't know the burdens I am bearing!"* This is where courage and faith collide. When we come to the Lord in confidence and pray for what we're asking, remember who you're talking to — the one and only true God, creator of all things. The one who formed you in your mother's womb.

Let me pause and reach out to you if you feel trapped by feelings of anger, hurt, or disappointment from someone who has hurt you in any way. I invite you to ask God to remove that hurt and replace it with His love and compassion. Although it is hard, I urge you to seek God's teaching to "Get rid of all bitterness, rage, anger, harsh words, and slander as well as all types of evil behavior. Instead, be kind to each other, be tenderhearted, and forgive one another just as God, through Christ, has forgiven you." (Ephesians 4:31-32) There was a time when I was so deeply hurt, I wasn't sure if I could ever forgive. It took time, that's for sure! But consider how when someone offends us, they are off living their life as if nothing has happened—not caring, or perhaps not even realizing –the depth of the wounds they caused in us. So, then, it is ourselves who continue to allow the hurt to affect us and render in us a downtrodden heart. I've learned an important lesson in life about forgiveness. It is a gift to ourselves to forgive!

Take refuge, my friend, in the loving arms of Christ, who bore our pain for us and redeems us. Relish in the joy of God's love, faithfulness, and assurance. As our favorite pastor recently said, "Maybe you've been checked out for so long you wonder if he'll even take your call! You want to repent but struggle to believe he'll accept you. You wonder if he'll hear your cry for help. Then you realize he's been there the whole time just waiting for you." Repent of holding onto unforgiveness. Take ahold of God's grace (forgiveness) and mercy (withholding punishment). "The Lord is not slow to fulfill his promise as some count slowness, but is patient toward you, not wishing that any should perish, but that all should reach repentance." (2 Peter 3:9)

Does God, all-knowing and faithful, always answer our prayers as we would choose them to be answered? Sometimes, answers to our prayers are not the ones we were searching for. Sometimes His answer is *yes*, sometimes it is *no,* and sometimes it is *wait*. This is the mystery that one day will be revealed to us. What we *do* know is that our Heavenly Father promises that He is with us. There are times when God prunes our lives, times when he multiplies, times he gives, and times he takes away.

There was a period in my life of about ten years where I had been an independent contractor for a direct sales company. The people I worked with for so long had become like family to me! It was a time of great fun, growth, travel, and excitement! Dearest of friendships were born across the country, one by one. We learned together, struggled together, laughed, and celebrated together, even cried together. We shared life! For a long time, my position with them became my identity. I couldn't imagine doing anything else until one day, I saw it slipping away. Everything I had known was coming to an end, and then it was gone.

Honestly, now, looking back, I realize I went through somewhat of an identity crisis. Who was I? I didn't recognize myself anymore. I experienced self-doubt, yearning for connection, craving affirmation, and seeking to find my place in the world. I had been held in high esteem, a leader, a sought-after speaker, and trainer, and now my heart was heavy. My confidence had waned. I disappointed others and myself. I felt as though I was a complete victim of my circumstances. My joy was sapped out of me. I cried. I wept. I felt bitter resentment and carried a chip on my shoulder, blaming others.

Sometimes, when we are at our lowest points in life, we are so low that the only direction is to look up. In my yearning for consolation, I turned to my Bible for wisdom, comfort, and perhaps guidance. But what I came to read in the book of James really perplexed me! "Consider it pure joy, my brothers and sisters, whenever you face trials of many kinds because you know the testing of your faith produces perseverance. Let perseverance finish its work so that you may be mature and complete, not lacking anything." (James 1:2-4)

Well! What was I to make of that? How could I find joy in my sadness and heavy heart? I'll be honest, this took me some time to swallow. I'm not just talking about these feelings for just a week or two; it was over a year. It's the next verse that helped pull me out of my slump when I finally came back to the only one who could rescue me from my pit. "If any of you lacks wisdom, you should ask God, who gives generously to all without finding fault, and it will be given to you." (James 1:5)

Let me tell you, I had to pull myself up by the bootstraps and ask him for the wisdom I was lacking, and pieces started to come together. I was persevering. I grew in my faith. I stopped feeling sorry for myself. I reminded myself of the only one who cared deeply and completely for me and would never forsake me. I drew near to God, searching for answers. In my deep despair, the Lord showed me my identity is *not of this world*, but *as a child of His*.

It became clear to me that our identity is not who we are in this world but who He is in this world.

"Rejoice always, pray without ceasing, give thanks in all circumstances; for this is the will of God in Christ Jesus for you." (1 Thes 15:16-18) Notice this verse refers to giving thanks "in" all circumstances, not "for" all circumstances. There will be trials in this world, but God is with us in the valleys of life. Also, note the instruction we're taught in this verse. It is broken into three actions we're to take as believers: rejoice, pray, and give thanks.

Well, if only I could always remember to do that – in that order! How easy it is to pray first, and then only if we get the answer we want, do we then give thanks and rejoice. No, God tells us to *rejoice first — then* pray without ceasing. Notice it doesn't say pray just once or when you feel like it. It says to *pray without ceasing*! Ah, and then to give thanks. Ought we then thank Him for the answer we didn't want? Remember that He is with us always, in and through the good and the bad. In this world, we will have trouble. We need to look up and know that God is in this life with us for the long haul. He is all-knowing and powerful. You *will* see a light at the end of the tunnel — it is Him, ready for you to come to him, sit with Him awhile, lean in, and trust Him. He is the Lord Jesus Christ, the Father of all mercies and God of all comfort, who comforts us in the midst of our troubles.

If you are a parent, guardian, aunt, uncle, or teacher, surely you know that when you discipline a child, it is only for their ultimate good — out of love and concern for their future. Likewise, out of love and concern for our future, our Heavenly Father will discipline us, make our path straight, and teach us to be holy as He is holy. After all, He is our eternal Father, having adopted us as his own when He drew us near to Him and we placed our faith in Jesus. There will be times when our choices have consequences, and we will learn from them. "And have you forgotten the exhortation that addresses you as sons? 'My son, do not regard lightly the discipline of the Lord, nor be weary when reproved by him.'" (Hebrews 12:5)

It's that last part, "when reproved by him," that can be hard. Sometimes, we make choices that are not according to God's will for us. And in hindsight, we can see it clearly. And yes, there are consequences. I know I have suffered consequences from making poor decisions, which resulted in a mess! When we make decisions and act out of God's will for us, we will likely have unpleasant consequences. When we discipline our children, we are doing it to teach them because we love them. When my kids were in high school, I worked from home for many years. They grew accustomed to being able to call me if they forgot their homework, their lunch, their uniform for practice, whatever it was. I realized while I didn't want them to go without what they needed, they weren't learning anything by my continuing to rescue them. They needed to face the consequences of their forgetfulness and take responsibility for their own actions or inaction. And guess what? They persevered. They learned. They grew. They became wiser.

Reflection Questions

When might you have witnessed God show up in your life, when least expected?

_____

_____

_____

_____

Where is God guiding you on your journey of 'being made holy'?

_____

_____

_____

_____

Where, or with whom, might the Holy Spirit be nudging you to replace bitterness, rage, anger, or unforgiveness with kindness, tenderheartedness, and forgiveness?

_____

_____

_____

_____

Courageously Step Out

Step Out

Courage in the Midst

"Have I not commanded you? Be strong and courageous. Do not be afraid; do not be discouraged, for the Lord your God will be with you wherever you go."
Joshua 1:9

There is a friend who is suffering through a debilitating fight with cancer. On social media, he continues to grip his followers, teaching us all a much deeper, greater understanding of faith, with encouragement and wisdom in his words – all in the midst of his weakness. Daily, he demonstrates how to conquer doubt, eradicate fear, and denounce failure. Just the other day, he posted, "Whether life right now is easy or hard, make the distinct choice to **choose joy every morning**. It will create a difference in your mind as drastic as night and day."

His attitude personifies Philippians 4:8. "Finally, brothers, whatever is true, whatever is honorable, whatever is just, whatever is pure, whatever is lovely, whatever is commendable, if there is any excellence, if there is anything worthy of praise, think about these things." That's courageous joy! A joy deep-seated in faith, unwavering.

Sometimes, we waver in our faith. We wonder why hard times have come our way or why we're being treated the way we are by an employer, a friend, or a family member. But we know God is with us through it all and cares very deeply. "Beloved, do not be surprised at the fiery trial when it comes upon you to test you as though something strange were happening to you. But rejoice insofar as you share Christ's sufferings, that you may also rejoice and be glad when his glory is revealed. If you are insulted for the name of Christ, you are blessed because the Spirit of glory and of God rests upon you." (1 Peter 4:12-14)

Take courage, my friend! Courage is foundational to being a Christian. Author Bill Hybels shares in his book, <u>Who You Are When No One's Looking</u>, "It takes courage to begin a walk with Christ, to reach out your hand and trust him. It takes courage to lead a life of obedience to Christ. It takes courage to be moral and build significant relationships with your spouse, children, and friends. It takes courage to expand a business, change your major, or start a new career. It takes courage to leave home or to go back home. Courage – we all need it, and God wants us to have it." To this day, we are told in the New Testament to "be on your guard; stand firm in the faith; be courageous; be strong." (1 Corinthians 16:13)

Sometimes, God calls us to step out in faith and trust him completely with what He is asking us to do. Consider Joshua, whom the Lord called upon to lead the Israelites across the Jordan into the promised land following the death of Moses. The Lord commanded Joshua not once, not twice, but three times to be strong and courageous! He would need to cross the Jordan when it was at flood stage and the water was fast flowing. "Be strong and courageous because you will lead these people to inherit the land I swore to their ancestors to give them. Be strong and very courageous. Be careful to obey all the laws my servant Moses gave you. Do not turn from it to the right or to the left, that you may be successful wherever you go." And again, he said to Joshua, "Have I not commanded you? Be strong and courageous. Do not be afraid; do not be discouraged, for the Lord your God will be with you wherever you go." (Joshua 1:6-9 NIV) The Jordan was fast-flowing, at flood stage, and approximately 100 feet wide. But God told Joshua, "As soon as the priests who carry the ark of the Lord — the Lord of all the earth — set foot in the Jordan, its waters flowing downstream will be cut off and stand up in a heap." (Joshua 3:13) And so when they came to cross the Jordan which was dangerously at flood stage, "*as soon as* the priests who carried the ark reached the Jordan and *their feet touched the water's edge*, the water from upstream stopped flowing. It piled up in a heap a great distance away, at a town called Adam in the vicinity of Zarethan, while the water flowing down to the sea of Arabah (that is, the Dead Sea) was completely cut off. So the people crossed over opposite Jericho. The priests who carried the ark of the covenant of the Lord stopped in the middle of the Jordan and stood on dry ground, while all Israel passed by until the whole nation had completed the crossing on dry ground." (Italics mine, Joshua 3:11-17 NIV). Pretty incredible, right? Imagine the **overwhelming joy** once they passed through to the other side!

But wait - what did the priests have to do first? They had to bravely **step into the water** to engage God's mighty power to stop the raging waters and hold them back for all the Israelites to pass through. What might God be prompting you to do, and you're sidestepping along, waiting for God to make the first move? Perhaps He is waiting for YOU to take the first step out in faith! When God gave us the spelling list of words in answer to our prayers, note that the last Word on that list was 'try.' God wants us to take that first step in faith! He lights the next step for us. He doesn't lead us astray. Prayerfully seek what the Lord is asking you to do. He will never ask us to do something that would harm ourselves or others. You will sense a small whisper or nudging if it is in His will.

When we step out in our faith, God shows up in big ways!

In the book of Daniel, we learn that Daniel defied the king of Babylon by not obeying the king's order not to petition any god other than the king himself. And this was punishable by an ordinance that such individuals shall be cast into a den of lions. Daniel knew he was to bow down to no other god or king than the one true God, so as it was ordered, Daniel was cast into the lion's den! When the king returned, expecting to see Daniel's body crushed and devoured by the lions, history reveals, "As he came near to the den where Daniel was, he cried out in a tone of anguish. The king declared to Daniel, 'O Daniel, servant of the living God, has your God, whom you serve continually, been able to deliver you from the lions?'" (Daniel 6:20) "He delivers and rescues; he works signs and wonders in heaven and on earth, he who has saved Daniel from the power of the lions." (Joshua 6:27) Oh, but to know the depth of God's mighty power over this world!

In what way might God be encouraging you to "Be strong and courageous. Do not be afraid; do not be discouraged, for the Lord your God will be with you wherever you go"?

Perfect in Weakness

"Likewise, the Spirit helps us in our weakness. For we do not know what to pray for as we ought, but the Spirit himself intercedes for us with groanings too deep for words."

Romans 8:26

Now, there's a strange combination of words. *Perfect in weakness* – really? When I first came across this topic in the Bible, I was convinced the Lord had intentions of turning my weaknesses into perfection. So, I anxiously read on to see just how this might come about! Well, in reading and rereading the passage, it became clear the Lord was still renewing my mind and teaching me through His Word. He taught me a *completely* different lesson!

A dear friend of ours had been in a terrible car accident. For a time, it was not clear whether he would even survive. As the days wore on in the hospital, several visitors came to see him. While he lay there still and hardly able to move, he shared his faith with many. He spoke of how great our God is, how grateful he was for the Lord being with him throughout this tragedy and blessing him in the midst of his pain and agony. Indeed, God's love shone perfectly through our friend's weakest moment.

God's power is made strong when we are weak, not in our own strength, no, as we might be tempted to think more of ourselves than we ought as if it were of *our own* doing. Stop to think for a moment or two. What could you accomplish today that would defy worldly logic but show God's mighty hand at work? What would your friends say as they see you do the seemingly impossible — that they know you couldn't do on your own — that it's only made possible by God? It is true. "I can do all things through Him who strengthens me." (1 Phil 4:13)

His grace is sufficient to take us through all suffering and trials here on earth. It is hard, really hard sometimes, to go a different way than the world, like trying to paddle upstream on a Colorado whitewater rafting expedition! "But Jesus looked at them and said, "With man this is impossible, but with God all things are possible." (Matthew 19:26)

Have you ever heard people refer to something as a *thorn in their side*? People often use this expression casually, referring to something or someone nagging them in their lives, such as a recurring physical injury, a situation, or a difficult person. This expression came about from the predicament Paul shares in 2 Corinthians.

Having received many visions and revelations from the Lord, Paul speaks of refraining from boasting "so that no one may think more of me than he sees in me or hears from me. So, to keep me from becoming conceited because of the surpassing greatness of the revelations, a thorn was given me in the flesh, a messenger of Satan to harass me, to keep me from becoming conceited. I pleaded with the Lord three times, begging it to leave me. But he said to me, "Grace is sufficient for you, for my power is made perfect in weakness.' Therefore, I will boast all the more gladly of my weaknesses, so that the power of Christ may rest upon me." (2 Corinthians 12:6-9) When Paul says *he was given a thorn*, its theological meaning is *for a beneficial purpose.*

Beneficial purpose? I'm sure none of us like the sound of that, knowing it's regarding an affliction or weakness. And then I am reminded of our friend who survived his accident. Divine power intercedes for us in our human weakness. We cannot accomplish on our own what we can when Christ is brought into the fold. In His empowerment, things may seem impossible for us, but they are possible through Christ. Indeed, the cross Jesus bore is the greatest example of power in weakness.

Hmmm. Now, there's something to ponder! Notice that Paul confronted the Lord, "Three times I pleaded with the Lord about this, " saying the thorn in the flesh should leave him. How many times have you heard the expression referring to something as a thorn in one's side? What thorn in *your* side might God be trying to reveal to you? If we could do magnificent works on our own without this thorn in our side, who would get the credit? You? Or God? Read verse 2 Corinthians 12:9 again. *What* is made perfect in weakness? God's power!

By looking at our weaknesses with a fresh set of eyes, we might be able to reassess our weaknesses — not as an excuse or reason to sap joy from our lives, but as a tool to be used by God for *His power* to be made perfect *through us*. After all, how can God's power be revealed through us if we do not come from a position of weakness?

From this viewpoint, we can understand Paul's next declaration in verse 10. "For the sake of Christ, then, I am content with weaknesses, insults, hardships, persecutions, and calamities. For when I am weak, then I am strong." Have you ever considered boasting all the more gladly of your weaknesses? It does put a new perspective on it!

What has the Lord put in your heart that, if it came about, would truly bring you great joy? What might be holding you back? What might the Lord be asking you to do, although you may feel inadequate or unqualified? What weakness of yours might God be patiently waiting to use to have *His power* made perfect through you? Embrace your weakness with courage. Allow God's power to be made perfect through you.

Romans 8:26 says, "The Spirit helps us in our weakness for we do not know what to pray as we ought, but the Spirit himself intercedes for us with groanings too deep for words." Pray for God to help you break through the barriers that only he can penetrate.

God shows up in even the smallest details of life.

When I was a young mom of three (our youngest had not been born yet), I volunteered on a pregnancy hotline. In those days, pregnancy tests weren't conveniently available to buy on store shelves. So, we offered free pregnancy tests and guidance anonymously. We lived near the University of La Crosse, Wisconsin at the time. One day, a young couple called and came to the house to conduct a pregnancy test. Well, it came out positive. They were young and in love, and they knew they wanted to get married, but they also knew that their parents would not be happy with them as it would change the course of their lives immensely.

I shared with them facts about their baby's development, comforted them, and shared how much joy my babies had brought us and our parents. God's timing is not always our timing, and we are responsible for the choices we make. God helps us through it. I remember telling them that this child was in their hands and they were the only ones to protect and nurture this life. I was powerless to affect their decision as they were contemplating abortion.

"As you do not know the path of the wind, or how the body is formed in a mother's womb, so you cannot understand the work of God, the Maker of all things." (Ecclesiastes 11:5) Sometimes in life, the choices we make change our path. But we also know when the Lord is our Savior, He is with us. And He will guide us as we follow Him and seek Him in all circumstances.

I want to pause here and wrap my arms around those of you who may have chosen abortion. I urge you to fall into the loving arms of Jesus. Ask for His forgiveness, and know **you are not only forgiven, but you are loved**! You are precious to Him! You are His beautiful child whom he loves dearly and offers you eternal life when you trust in Him.

My heart goes out to the many young women who have been hijacked by the lies of this world, hurt by the pain of judgmental eyes, pressure from peers, disdainful treatment by others, or even abandoned. Let God's unfailing love and mercy enlighten us all!

We are taught through God's Word to "Speak up for those who cannot speak for themselves, for the rights of all who are destitute." (Proverbs 31:8) We know every child created cannot speak for themselves while still in the womb, and we also know that God loves each of us dearly. "Are not five sparrows sold for two pennies? Yet not one of them is forgotten by God." (Luke 12:6) **Take heart, dear one! You are forgiven,** "as far as the East is from the West, so far has he removed our transgressions from us."

I prayed for this young couple as they left and for a long time afterward for them to decide to bring this child into the world. My heart ached not knowing the outcome. **Sometimes, the Lord just shows up, puts our weakness aside, and surprises us to our sheer delight!** About four years later, I was out with my kids, taking them Trick-or-Treating in the neighborhood. We got to one house, rang the bell, and a young mom opened the door. "Trick-or-Treat!" they shouted! As I thanked her and turned to leave, she asked me, "Are you the one that lives in the small blue house around the corner?" "Yes," I answered curiously. She looked familiar, but I couldn't place her. Then she opened the door wider, stepping aside, "Hi! This is our daughter. We had a girl. She's four now!"

Talk about a sudden swelling and throbbing of the heart! I had always wondered, and now the Lord was gracious enough to confirm for me that this young couple had decided to bring their baby into the world. I can't tell you how incompetent I felt when I was asked to sign up for a timeslot to take those phone calls on the hotline. I was always relieved when the hour came at the end of my shift.

Where I was weak, God was strong!

Prayer

Lord, you alone know the burdens and the weaknesses we bear. You know what we need before we ask you. You are in control.

We pray in confidence from the words of Ephesians 3:14-19: Lord, I bow my knees before you, Father, from whom every family in Heaven and on earth is named, that according to the riches of your glory may you grant that I be strengthened with power through your Spirit in my inner being so that Christ may dwell in my heart through faith—that I, being rooted and grounded in love, may have strength to comprehend with all the saints what is the breadth and length and height and depth, and to know the love of Christ that surpasses knowledge, that I may be filled with all the fullness of God.

Amen

Courageous Joy!

"Delight yourself in the Lord, and He will give you the
desires of your heart."
Psalm 37:4

J esus uses a metaphor of remaining in the vine and bearing
fruit in His teaching of the fruit we bear as Christians. In the
book of Galatians, chapter 5, we're taught what the evidence
(fruit) of our faith is, as seen through the eyes of how we treat
others. This fruit results from having the Holy Spirit within us as
we follow Jesus. Ripe, beautiful, delicious fruit! They are love, joy,
peace, patience, kindness, goodness, faithfulness, gentleness,
and self-control.

Joy does not just happen! It is the result of a cultivated heart,
with the inner workings of the Holy Spirit, in following the
precepts of God. In your joy, you represent the salt of the earth,
a light on a hill to those who reside in the dark in this world, and
you are blessed!

Grab ahold of the days when you might get caught up in the
busyness of everyday life, bereft of the mindfulness of God's
awesome wonder. Stop and mindfully redirect your thoughts to
Jesus. While we are here on this earth, there is a wonderful peace
that only He alone can give. In times of trouble, turn to His
promise in the book of Philippians. "Do not be anxious about
anything, but in everything by prayer and supplication with
thanksgiving let your requests be made known to God. And the
peace of God, which surpasses all understanding, will guard your
hearts and your minds in Christ Jesus. Finally, brothers, whatever
is true, whatever is honorable, whatever is just, whatever is pure,

whatever is lovely, whatever is commendable, if there is any excellence, if there is anything worthy of praise, think about these things." (Phil 4:6-8)

In searching for joy, "Do not be conformed to this world, but be transformed by the renewal of your mind, that by testing you may discern what the will of God is, what is good and acceptable and perfect." Refer to the beginning of the book, where you wrote down some of the things the Lord has put in your heart that bring you joy. God placed the desires of your heart within you, and you honor Him when you carry them out for the good of others. He has uniquely equipped you with gifts from the Holy Spirit. Worship God joyfully through the use of your unique talents and abilities. Joyful work springs from your highest sense of purpose, service, and love! Allow the fullness of your uniqueness to honor God and serve others; in doing so, your Joy will overflow! Regardless of circumstances, you'll experience a more profound, sustainable joy — not a fleeting happiness but rather a special, rare, and sacred joy that we yearn for.

Step out in worship by serving others. Look and see what's going on around you, where you live, where you're at, to places where God is moving. Ask how you can help. How can you be a part of it? And step out for Jesus. Take in the joy you gain from serving Him through serving others. Receive the blessing from loving on others. Service is worship, sharing God's love with others. This is a connection point. Seek Him in Prayer—it changes our perspective! Instead of asking why this or that is happening, we begin to *thank Him* for seeing Him *work through* our current circumstances.

Choose Joy! Boldly step out in your faith. Let your light shine among others. Let your courage be mighty, and your joy be courageous and contagious! "Until now you have asked nothing in my name. Ask, and you will receive, that your joy may be full." (John 16:24) Remember, you have a God who loves you unconditionally, and He accepts you right where you are in your life. You don't need first to get your act together or your house in order before you come to the Lord. Come now, with a grateful and contrite heart, raw, with all your troubles and messiness of this world.

In our yearning for joy, seeking fellowship, and longing for peace, we have a God who says, just ask, and your joy will be complete. Yes, complete! And the beauty of it all is that in your joy, you make our heavenly Father's joy complete as well! We were created in His image to live courageously and joyfully in this world. Joy is God-centered. Worship God for who He is and what He's done. You will begin to find peace and joy in whatever circumstance you find yourself in. Jesus, in speaking to His disciples, told them, "As the Father has loved me, so have I loved you. Abide in my love. If you keep my commandments, you will abide in my love, just as I have kept my Father's commandments and abide in his love. These things I have spoken to you, and that your joy may be full." John 15:9-11

"These things I have spoken to you, that my joy may be in you, and that your joy may be full."
– Jesus

Prayer

Lord, you know my innermost being, my weaknesses, and my frailties. You are tender and merciful. Yet you still love me and long for me to be filled with joy. Lord, I confess I get distracted by the cares of life and regularly lose sight of your goodness.

If there is any unconfessed sin or any barrier that is between us that is hindering the flow of joy in my life, please reveal it to me so I can surrender it to you.

God of hope, fill me with all joy and peace in believing so that by the power of the Holy Spirit, I may abound in hope. Fill my heart, Lord, with unprecedented, sacred joy! Let me draw near with a true heart in full assurance of faith, with my heart sprinkled clean from an evil conscience and my body washed with pure water. Let me hold fast the confession of my hope without wavering, for he who promised is faithful. And let me consider how to stir up one another to love and good works.

Lord, cultivate me. Help me to remain in you, in your Word, in both faith and deed. Help me to see you beyond my own weaknesses. Give me endless courage and strength all the days of my life. Build in me courage and faith like that of Daniel. And may this hope and assurance birth a new lift in my step, an outward expression of joy springing forth from my heart. And yes, Lord, let me live out this life with Courageous Joy!

Amen

Reflection Questions

What weakness of yours might you reassess as a tool to be used by God for His power to be revealed through you?

_____

_____

_____

_____

God knit you in your mother's womb and nestled the desires of your heart deep inside you. What unique talents, abilities, and passions were created in you, which, when gripped with bold courage and faith, will open your heart to the joy you're searching for?

_____

_____

_____

_____

God told Joshua three times to be courageous and strong. Where has God shed light on the next step for you?

_____

_____

_____

_____

About the Author

At the age of nineteen, while horseback riding on an unusually warm January day, Julie McCarthy prayerfully asked, "Lord, is this everything there is to life? Or is there more? Am I missing something? Please show me." Discovering the answers transformed her life — forever! Julie's thirst to continue to draw nearer to God has fueled her desire to lead women in their journey of learning God's word and applying it in everyday life.

Julie is an accomplished entrepreneur and speaker. Julie holds a master's degree in Organizational Leadership from the University of Northwestern — St. Paul. She has been married to her husband, Guy, for over 40 years. They have four adult children and six grandchildren. Her dearest titles are wife, mom, grandma, and friend.

Please Leave a Review on Amazon

Thank you for reading ***Courageous Joy!***
If you enjoyed reading it and sharing our journey together, please be so kind to post a short review on Amazon.
Your support truly matters, and we deeply appreciate your feedback.

Notes

_____
_____
_____
_____
_____
_____
_____
_____
_____
_____
_____
_____
_____
_____
_____
_____
_____
_____
_____
_____

Made in the USA
Monee, IL
26 August 2024

63958744R00046